Kathy Rucker

Possum Trot

The Birth of a Ghost Town

Salamander Street

PLAYS

PB ISBN: 9781068233432

10 9 8 7 6 5 4 3 2 1

Further copies of this publication can be purchased from
www.salamanderstreet.com

Wordville

To Hal and Hannah, with gratitude and love. Always.

Possum Trot was first performed at The Theatre at the Tabard in London from 12 November until 29 November 2025.
The cast was as follows:

Maxine	**Sarah Berger**
Duane	**Todd Bryce**
Pru	**Dani Arlington**
Jeremiah	**Nikolas Salmon**
Billie	**Neve Francis**
Writer	**Kathy Rucker**
Director	**Scott Le Crass**
Producer	**Kevin Nolan**
Set & Costume Designer	**Reuben Speed**
Lighting Designer	**Joseph Bryant**
Composer & Sound Designer	**Hannah Bracegirdle**
Stage Manager	**Rachael Corrigan**
Production Assistant	**Réka Sztrinkó**

THE CAST

Sarah Berger | Maxine

Sarah is an actress, director, producer and artist.

Her long career as an actress has included three seasons at The Royal Shakespeare Company, five West End shows, national and international tours ranging from Shakespeare and Coward to Ayckbourn and countless tv appearances.

She has just completed a National tour of *Death Comes to Pemberley*, playing Lady Catherine de Bourgh.

As a director Sarah has directed seven premieres of new plays in London, Edinburgh and New York. In 2018 she directed a bilingual production of *Macbeth* at the state theatre of Kyrgyzstan.

Sarah founded the So and So Arts Club in 2012 and has produced 80 rehearsed readings, two repertory seasons of new plays and six international festivals. In addition, she produced Kathy Rucker's play *Darling* at the Hope Theatre in Islington.

Sarah has been nominated for the Guilder Coigney international award for Women in Theatre twice, she was a finalist in the Global Women Awards 2018 and is an ambassador for the Rahela Trust, a charity that seeks to help women in Afghanistan complete their education. She won a cultural award for her work in Central Asia and in Kazakhstan for her work alongside the Ardi disabled theatre company.

Todd Boyce | Duane

Todd is best known for playing series regular Stephen Reid in ITV's *Coronation Street*.

Further television credits include: *The Crown, Sherlock, Mr Selfridge, Beaver Falls, A Spy Among Friends, Legacy, Alex Rider, High and Dry, Billionaire Boy, The Game, Hollyoaks, Spooks, Two Wheels Through Terror, Adventures Inc, Broken News, Comfort Zone, Discovery, Hear the Silence, Home Farm Twins, Hostile Waters, Macready & Daughter, TheUnexpected Mrs Pollifax, My Beautiful Son, Out of the Past, Space Race, The Ruby Ring, Unfinished Business, Melba, Fields of Fire.*

Theatre credits include: *Death Comes to Pemberley* (Mill at Sonning/UK Tour), *Sleuth* (Bill Kenwright Productions/UK Tour), *Mother Goose* (Little Wolf Entertainment), *The Exorcist* (Birmingham Rep/Phoenix Theatre), *Late Company* (Trafalgar Studios), *Last of the Boys* (Southwark Playhouse), *Fixer* (High Tide), *Midnight Cowboy* (Edinburgh Assembly Rooms), *Ball Boys* (Griffin Theatre Company), *Burn This, Doctor Faustus, The Normal Heart* (Sydney Theatre Company), *Gentlemen Prefer Blondes, Key Largo* (New Moon Theatre Company),

Glyn and It (Yvonne Arnaud), *Hamlet* (Young Vic/Tour), *Lovers from Hell* (Oval Theatre), *On Top of the World* (Croydon Warehouse), *The Exonerated* (Riverside Studios), *The Women of Lockerbie* (Orange Tree Theatre), *West Coast Romeo* (Harvest Theatre Company), *Who's Afraid of Virginia Woolf?* (South Australian Theatre Company).

Film credits include: *The Batman, Kingsman 3: The Outfit, Murder on the Orient Express, Anamorphosis, Denial, Fantastic Beasts and Where to Find Them, Reindeer in the Mist, Everest, In Clear Sight, Kick Ass 2, The Filmmaker's Son, Kon Tiki, The Gatekeeper, Penelope, Flyboys, Charlie and the Chocolate Factory, The Life and Death of Peter Sellers, The Final Curtain, Hills like White Elephants, Spy Game, Jefferson in Paris, Blue Ice, The Delinquents, The Punisher, Great Expectations, Susannah's Dreaming, The Labyrinth.*

Dani Arlington | Pru

Dani is an Actor/Director from Teesside. She gained a full scholarship to train at Mountview Academy of Theatre Arts, London and also HB Studio, New York.

Her theatre credits include, *Prima Facie* (Broadway and West End— Harold Pinter Theatre), *Tiny beautiful things* (Somerset House) *Saint Maud* and *The Savage* (Live Theatre), *Tinder Surprise* (Arcola Theatre), *HER* (The Arts Theatre), *The Flowers o' Edinburgh* (The Finborough), *Studs* and *A Pair of Beauties* (Hull Truck Theatre National tour), *Be My Baby* (Gala Theatre), *Third Floor, The Comedy of Errors* (The Cockpit), *The Women* (Jackson's Lane).

Dani's TV credits include a returning role for CBBC's *The Dumping Ground*, Anna Marsh in *Doctors* (BBC), and various commercials.

Director/Assistant Director credits include *Mary & Pam* at The New Diorama, *Darling* at The Hope Theatre, *The Fulstow Boys* UK tour by Gordon Steel. Director credits: *Crumbling Walls* and *The Speaker* at Live Theatre.

Nikolas Salmon | Jeremiah

Nik trained at Mountview Academy of Theatre Arts.

Previous Theatre credits include: *The Totalitarians* (English Theatre Frankfurt), *For King and Country* (The Southwark Playhouse), *Into Battle* (Greenwich Theatre), *She Stoops to Conquer* and *All's Well That End's Well* (Changeling Theatre, UK Tour).

Film/TV credits include: *The Ministry of Ungentlemanly Warfare* (LionsGate Films), *Eastenders* (BBC), *260 Days* (Arramis Films Inc).

Neve Francis | Billie

Neve Francis is a Liverpool-bred, London-based queer actor and improviser. Graduating from ArtsEd in 2024, she has since appeared in *Living Dying Dead* (Playing Dead Theatre), *Possum Trot* (The Theatre at the Tabard), and continues to perform as a swing in Inventive Productions immersive theatre shows.

THE CREATIVES

Kathy Rucker | Writer

Kathy Rucker is an award-winning American playwright whose work has been produced in the US and the UK, captivating audiences with sharp wit, emotional depth, and timely explorations of contemporary issues.

Her play *Crystal Springs* premiered at London's Park Theatre and San Francisco's Eureka Theatre, earning the London Independent Story Prize for Best Stage Play. The Independent called it "an acutely intelligent play about cyberbullying... highly recommended." Her play *Darling*, produced at the Hope Theatre in London, was nominated for the Standing Ovation Award.

Other plays include *Sultan's Battery* (Fresh Baked Theatre Company, Los Angeles); *Turing Tested* and *Beautiful Scar* (a finalist for the Heideman Award at the Humana Festival, Louisville, Kentucky); *Done There, Been That* (Bierkeller Theatre, Bristol); *Maxine* (Barons Court Theatre, London). Her work has been showcased at the Great Plains Theatre Conference, Last Frontier Theatre Conference, and the Sewanee Writers Conference.

Before her playwriting career, Kathy worked as a producer in the film industry. She lives in California with her husband and daughter and is a graduate of the University of California, Berkeley.

Scott Le Crass | Director

Scott was born in Bristol, grew up in Birmingham, trained as an actor at Arts Ed and was a director on the Birmingham Rep's first Foundry Programme. In 2022, he completed the National Theatre Director's Course.

He is an Associate Director for Pleasure Dome Theatre Company and has directed all their productions to date.

Scott directed the Off Com award-winning digital revival of *Rose* by Martin Sherman starring Maureen Lipman (Hope Mill Theatre/Sky Arts/Broadway HD). In 2023 he was nominated for Best Creative West End Debut at The Stage Awards for his production of *Rose*. In 2022, he received an Off West End and Broadway World nomination for Best Director for *Rose*. In 2024 *Rose* won an Off West End award for Best Solo Performance.

Credits include: Director- *Rose* (West End), *Cut The Crap* starring Sharon Osbourne (West End), *Elmer* (UK and International Tour/Sell A Door), *Sid* (Arts Theatre and UK Tour), *Toxic* (HOME, Manchester/UK tour), *Buff* (UK tour), *Nostos* (Southwark Playhouse), *Marshmallow Me* (UK tour), *Second Summer of Love* (UK tour), *The Witches* (Watford Palace), *Alice in Wonderland* (Old, Rep, Birmingham), *Jab* (Finborough Theatre/ Park Theatre), *Rose* (Hope Mill Theatre/Park Theatre), *Country Music* (Omnibus Theatre), *Zanna Don't* (Old Joint Stock Theatre), *Shooting Star, The Musical* (The Two Brewers, Clapham), *The Mad Gay King* (King's Head Theatre), *My Life As A Cowboy* (Omnibus Theatre), *Did You Mean To Fall Like That* (Edinburgh Fringe), *Pillock* (Contact Theatre/Edinburgh Fringe), *Wormholes* (Omnibus Theatre), *The Railway Children* (OVO Roman Theatre), *My Dear Aunty Nell* (Tour), *Merboy* (Omnibus Theatre), *Thirsty* (Vault Festival), *Twelfth Night* (East London Shakespeare Festival), *I Couldn't Do Your Job* (Pleasance Theatre, London/Queens Theatre, Hornchurch), *If You Love Me This Might Hurt* by Matty May (Camden People's Theatre), *Education, Education Karaoke* (Camden People's Theatre), *Darling* (Hope Theatre), *Kicked in the Sh**ter* (Hope Theatre/ Theatre in The Mill, Bradford).

Kevin Nolan | Producer

Kevin is Managing Director of Sibearita Productions Ltd., a London-based theatre and media production company dedicated to creating commercial, creative and critically successful new work that advocates for marginalised groups and individuals.

After a 20-year career in technology research and consulting, Kevin became a full-time theatre producer in 2022. Prior to this, he served as Associate Producer on several productions including Offie-Award Winning *Country Music* by Simon Stephens (Omnibus Theatre, 2019).

Kevin's first solo production, *Buff* by Ben Fensome (Pleasance, July 2023), achieved outstanding critical and commercial success at the Edinburgh Fringe Festival, winning a Playbill 'Pick of the Fringe' award. *MANikin* by Nathan Scott-Dunn, co-produced with Saltire Sky Theatre, won Best Drama at the Edinburgh Fringe Derek Awards 2024.

Kevin has also served as Production Manager on award-nominated shows including *Jab* by James McDermott (Finborough Theatre, March 2024; Park Theatre, April 2025) and *Wormholes* by Emily Jupp (Omnibus Theatre, August 2024).

Reuben Speed | Designer

Reuben is an award-winning designer (2023 Off West End Costume designer). He trained at the Royal Central School of Speech and Drama.

Previous design work includes *La Boheme* (Regents Opera, UK and French Tour), *Speakeasy, with Karen and Gorka* (The Adelphie & UK Tour) *The Mad Ones* (Electric Press Productions), *Be More Chill*, *Xanna Don't* (Old Joint Stock), *Into The Woods* (ArtsEd), *Everybody Dance* (The London Palladium & UK Tour), *I'm Gonna Marry You Tobey Maguire* (Southwark Playhouse) *Ushers The Musical* (James Steel Productions), *Jane Eyre*, *Sister Act*, *Carrie* (Urdang Academy), *The Wizard of OZ, 9 to 5* (Emil Dale Academy), *A Very Very Bad Cinderella* (The Other Palace Studio), *Kin A New Musical* (Theatro Technis), *Boy Out The City* (The Lyric Theatre and UK Tour), *Trompe L'Oeil* (The Other Palace), *Halls The Musical* (The Turbine), *Wet Feet, Betty Blue Eyes, Peace in Our Time*. Lional Barts musical revival of *Blitz!*, *Tom Brown's School Days*, *Whistle Down The Wind*, *Hello Again*, *Lucky Stiff* (Union Theatre), *Dr Faustus* (The Southwark Playhouse,

Lazarus Theatre, Offie Nom), *Hello Jerry, Coloured Lights* and *Showcase* (Royal Academy of Music), *Legally Blonde, Addams Family, Work It, Love and Information* and *Bitchboxer* (Performers Manchester).

Reuben has designed for The New Vic Theatre in Staffordshire with their youth theatre verbatim musical *High Flyers*.

Joseph Bryant | Lighting Designer

Joe is a London-based Lighting Designer and Technician working across the Live Entertainment Industry, specialising in Theatre Making and Set Electrics. He has received training from various institutions, including The Brit School and The Royal Central School of Speech and Drama.

Joe utilizes his strong technical skill set and keen eye for detail to deliver high-quality, emotionally captivating pieces of storytelling.

Hannah Bracegirdle | Sound Designer

Hannah is a freelance Sound Designer who enjoys working in a collaborative nature. She graduated from The Bristol Old Vic Theatre School in 2022.

Theatrical credits include: Sound Designer on *Gobby Girls: 11% Club* (Gobby Girl Productions), *WANTED* (Bush Productions), *Macbeth, Taming of the Shrew* and *Blithe Spirit* (HER Productions), *Animal Farm* (Litchfield Garrick), *Spamalot* (Thin Air Theatre Company USA), *Identities* and *Climax* (Close to Home Productions), *Burning Down the Horse* (Fishing for Chips), *My Dear Aunty Nell* (Camdens Peoples Theatre) and *Caligula and the Sea* (The Vaults).

Sound Associate on *Peak Stuff* (ThickSkin) and Sound Assistant on *What about me?* (Salford Community Leisure with Breaking Barriers).

Rachael Corrigan | Stage Manager

Rachael is a theatre technician and stage manager from London. She has a degree in Technical Theatre from St Mary's University in Twickenham. She has worked across multiple fringe festivals, comedy shows and theatre productions.

She has previously worked at Theatre at the Tabard as the Stage Manager for *On Demand* and Deputy Stage Manager for *The Count of Monte Cristo*.

Réka Sztrinkó | Production Assistant

Réka was born and raised in Hungary. She graduated with an MA in Theatre Studies from Kőroli Góspór University, Budapest and moved to London to put her knowledge into practice and pursue her dream of working in the theatre industry.

She has been working in the West End since 2023. *Possum Trot* marks her first professional role in Production Management.

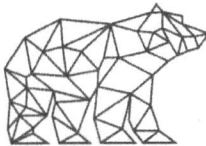

SIBEARITA
PRODUCTIONS

Kathy Rucker

Possum Trot

CHARACTERS:

MAXINE

Woman, 65

PRUDENCE

Daughter of Maxine, 43

JEREMIAH

Husband of Prudence, 42

BILLIE

Daughter of Jeremiah and Prudence, 18

DUANE

Widower, neighbor, 65

TIME:

Present day

PLACE:

Possum Trot, a very small town in Nebraska, USA

Setting: The play opens inside an old diner. There is a bar with a dozen stools. A few wooden tables and worn, red Naugahyde chairs are scattered about. Above the bar is a collection of old beer mugs. On the wall is a large neon sign advertising beer, a bulletin board with photos and announcements, a large menu including the day's specials which never change, and a sign that says 'Coldest Beer in Town!'

SCENE 1

The lights are off in the diner but we can hear the sound of people talking, music, laughter, dishes clanging, orders being barked. MAXINE, dressed in black, enters, taking off her raincoat, shaking her umbrella before putting it in the bucket near the door. The room is now silent. She turns the lights on, the neon sign flickers. She thumps the sign and it steadies. She goes behind the counter, kisses her two fingers, and gently taps a framed photo of her late husband.

MAXINE: (*to the photo*) Hon, you should be happy you died in the summer.

She opens a new can of coffee, puts the grounds into the coffee maker.

MAXINE: What a mess today.

She pours water into the coffee maker.

MAXINE: The rain has been vicious and the thunder cracked so loud, my dentures rattled. Then Jeremiah slipped in the mud and almost tipped poor Burt's casket upside down.

She goes into the back room and brings out bread, mayonnaise, sliced meat and cheese. She begins making sandwiches.

MAXINE: Sarah screeched, of course. Father Bob calmed her down. She was as white as a ghost when the casket tipped, but poor Jeremiah. He felt bad. I could tell. He was biting his lip.

We hear the sound of a rooster.

MAXINE: Yes, Charlie's still alive. Crazy bird.

She walks to the window and looks out, watching the rain.

MAXINE: (*looking out the window*) Your poor vegetable garden. It's gone feral, I'm afraid.

She walks back to the counter.

MAXINE: I heard Sarah say that she's thinking of moving to Lincoln to be with her sister. You can't blame her, though, she can't run that farm on her own. I mean, how could she ever go in the barn again, after finding him there alone that way? I know I couldn't.

BILLIE and JEREMIAH enter the diner. JEREMIAH takes off his hat and hangs it on a wall hook.

BILLIE: You're wrong. The thunder was a good sign.

JEREMIAH: Good for who? You weren't holding Burt's casket.

BILLIE: That was so funny. Want to see? I've got it—

BILLIE gets out her phone.

JEREMIAH: —No thank you!

BILLIE: I should post it.

JEREMIAH: Don't you dare.

BILLIE hesitates and then pushes the 'Send' button on her phone.

BILLIE: Too late.

MAXINE looks at BILLIE's phone and gently laughs.

JEREMIAH: You, too?

BILLIE: I'm calling it—"Population five and dropping."

JEREMIAH: That's just great.

JEREMIAH surreptitiously takes a sip from a flask and puts it back in his pocket.

BILLIE: Anyway, the thunder and lightning mean that he's passed through the pearly gates—

JEREMIAH: —It's just weather, Billie. There's nothing religious about it.

BILLIE: I like to think it means that Burt's OK.

MAXINE: He's no longer in pain. But I'm not so sure about the heaven part.

BILLIE: How can you say that, Gram?

MAXINE: The church has a thing about people who, you know, who, uh—

BILLIE: —Oh my God, there shouldn't be such a stigma. We should talk about it. It's what happened.

MAXINE: The Church is against it, that's all I'm saying.

BILLIE: That's bullshit. Screw the Pope or whoever made up that lame-ass rule.

MAXINE: Language!

BILLIE: Sorry.

JEREMIAH helps MAXINE with the food. BILLIE is using her phone to shoot video of MAXINE making sandwiches.

JEREMIAH: (*to BILLIE*) Uh, right. Want a sandwich?

BILLIE: What do you have?

MAXINE: Baloney or baloney.

BILLIE: Nah, I'm not really hungry.

JEREMIAH: Suit yourself.

BILLIE: In fact, I think I have long Covid.

MAXINE: How could you have long Covid? You never had Covid.

BILLIE: I have all the symptoms.

BILLILE searches on her phone and tries to show her dad the Covid symptom website.

BILLIE: Here, see?

JEREMIAH: You don't have long Covid. Can you put that phone down for just a minute? God, I really hate those things.

BILLIE puts her earbuds in and scrolls her phone.

JEREMIAH: (*to MAXINE*) I'm going to pick up the supplies for the party today. Did you want to add anything to the list.

BILLIE: (*reading from her phone*)   Fatigue. Congestion. Body aches...

MAXINE: I'm not so sure that the party is a good idea.

BILLIE: —Cloudy brain. Nausea. Congested.

MAXINE: (*to BILLIE*) What did you have last month? Consumption, was it?

BILLIE: Scarlet fever.

MAXINE: (*to BILLIE*) Right.

JEREMIAH: The party is a great idea.

BILLIE: It was a really bad sore throat.

JEREMIAH: Fifty years is a long time, Max. It deserves a celebration. (*To BILLIE*) You don't have long Covid.

MAXINE: What if no one comes? Not much to celebrate then.

JEREMIAH: Every farmer within a fifty-mile radius will come. And probably some of those hunters who love your chili and cold beer.

MAXINE: But how can you pick up the supplies? Don't you have some corn to harvest?

JEREMIAH: The harvester is broken. I'm waiting for a part.

MAXINE: Waiting for a part... again?

JEREMIAH: It's old.

BILLIE: (*with her hand to her forehead*) Do I have a fever?

JEREMIAH: (*feeling BILLIE's forehead*) No. You're fine.

MAXINE: Where's Pru?

JEREMIAH: She had to do some errands.

The neon sign starts strobing again.

MAXINE: Now? She knew I needed her help.

JEREMIAH: (*noticing the strobing neon sign*) She'll be here. Is that beer sign on the fritz again?

JEREMIAH gives the neon sign a little tap. Nothing happens. MAXINE goes to the neon sign and gives it another whack.

Fixed.

MAXINE: She promised to make her coconut cake.

MAXINE stacks sandwiches on a plate. There are a lot of them.

MAXINE: Do you think this is enough?

BILLIE: Gram, it's just us. Sarah and her sister got a lift home. She said they were tired.

MAXINE: And Father Bob?

BILLIE: He drove them home.

MAXINE: The Andersons?

JEREMIAH: They moved to Florida last March, remember?

MAXINE: Bob Putnam should be here soon. He loves a good wake.

BILLIE: He's dead.

MAXINE: Oh, right.

MAXINE crosses herself. BILLIE opens a can of soda, drinks, belches.

MAXINE: Arnie Cooper?

BILLIE: Di—

MAXINE: —Don't!

BILLIE: Divorced. Gone.

MAXINE: Oh.

BILLIE: (*under her breath*) Fucking ghost town.

JEREMIAH goes to change the station on the radio.

MAXINE: Hands off the radio, mister!

JEREMIAH: I wanted to check the weather.

MAXINE: (*looking out the window*) It's raining.

JEREMIAH: I don't like the idea of Pru out there. The storm's getting worse.

DUANE enters the diner, dripping wet.

DUANE: (*to MAXINE*) Hey, Maxine. (*to JEREMIAH*) Jeremiah.

MAXINE: Hi, Duane. Do you want a sandwich?

DUANE: No, just the usual.

Maxine points to the clock.

MAXINE: It's 11a.m., Duane. Which usual?

DUANE: (*looking at the clock*) I'll take the 5p.m., please.

MAXINE grabs a can of beer from the refrigerator and gives it to him.

BILLIE: Hey, Duane.

DUANE: Billie, did you hear the one about the hungry clock?

MAXINE: It's a wake, Duane.

DUANE: Is it?

JEREMIAH: Burt Hollis.

DUANE: Good man.

DUANE lifts his beer in a toast.

DUANE: To Burt! God bless.

BILLIE: (*to DUANE, whispering*) What about the hungry clock?

DUANE: (*whispering*) It went back four seconds.

BILLIE: Ah, man. I'll give that a two.

DUANE: Just a two? OK, so this moth goes to see a podiatrist—

MAXINE: Really?

DUANE: It's a classic Norm McDonald joke.

MAXINE: No.

DUANE: (*whispering to BILLIE*) Another time.

DUANE winks at BILLIE.

MAXINE: Why weren't you there this morning?

DUANE: I don't do funerals.

MAXINE: You should have come. We mourn together.

BILLIE: (*showing her phone to DUANE*) Look what you missed.

JEREMIAH: I swear to God, Billie, I'm going to toss that fucking thing into the trash.

BILLIE: Whoa! Language!

MAXINE: Jeremiah.

JEREMIAH: (*to MAXINE*) Come on, she's always on that thing.

DUANE watches the video.

DUANE: (*laughing*) That is so Jeremiah!

JEREMIAH: What does that mean?

DUANE: Come on. Remember that time one of your cows got out during that big storm of '98. Poor creature got struck by lightning. You got some bad luck, that's all.

JEREMIAH: I'd say that it was the cow who had bad luck.

PRU enters the diner, holding a broken umbrella.

MAXINE: (*seeing PRU enter*) Well, finally.

PRU: Jeez, I didn't think I'd get here. A tree is down on Abbot Road. I had to take Route 17.

JEREMIAH: (*giving PRU a little hug*) Glad you made it safe. All good?

PRU: (*to JEREMIAH*) The north field is flooded.

JEREMIAH: Ah, shit. We just seeded there.

PRU: I know.

JEREMIAH: Twenty acres of sorghum.

PRU: I know, babe.

JEREMIAH: (*to himself*) You don't know.

PRU: What?

JEREMIAH: It's really bad.

PRU: (*to JEREMIAH*) Listen, there's something important I want to talk to you about.

MAXINE: The cake?

PRU: Oh, shit.

MAXINE: Really? I ask for one thing.

PRU: I'm sorry, Mom. I really am. I ran out of eggs and I didn't have time—

MAXINE: You raise chickens.

PRU: Uh, I ran out of flour.

MAXINE: You can do better than that.

PRU: I forgot.

MAXINE: Bingo.

PRU: I said I was sorry.

MAXINE: Folks are counting on me. On us.

PRU: So where is everyone?

MAXINE: Apparently, this is it.

PRU: Oh, that's sad.

MAXINE: We don't need a cake or sandwiches today. Just one beer evidently.

JEREMIAH grabs a beer, opens it and drinks.

MAXINE: Two beers.

DUANE: I hear some big aggie guys have been snooping around again.

MAXINE: Today is hard enough. Must we talk about that now?

MAXINE goes in the back.

DUANE: They're probably looking at Burt's place. It sure didn't take them long.

JEREMIAH: They're damn vultures.

PRU: It all depends on how you look at it.

JEREMIAH: Haven't they bought enough farms already? I mean, who's left?

DUANE: Burt should have sold, then maybe he'd still be alive.

JEREMIAH: (*to DUANE*) What the hell, Duane! You don't know that.

DUANE: Seems to me—

PRU: (*to DUANE*)—Have a sandwich, Duane. On the house.

MAXINE comes back to the counter.

BILLIE: (*yells*) I can't believe this. I've gone viral.

PRU: Please, not consumption again.

JEREMIAH: No, this time it's long Covid.

PRU: But she never had—

JEREMIAH: —that's correct.

BILLIE: Already 1,534 views of my funny funeral video!

PRU: What video?

BILLIE shows her Mom her casket-falling video.

PRU: (*cont.*) Possum underscore exposed? Is that you?

BILLIE: Yeah, that's me. I have over five thousand followers.

PRU: Oh, Billie.

JEREMIAH: Is that what I think it is? You posted it? Who can see that?

BILLIE: Everybody.

JEREMIAH: Everybody?

DUANE: It's pretty funny.

JEREMIAH: It makes me look like a damn fool.

PRU: Show your dad some respect, Billie.

BILLIE: It's what happened. I didn't make it up. I'm not trying to disrespect anybody. You'd know that if you looked at my work.

JEREMIAH: Your work?

BILLIE: Yeah. My work. My art.

PRU: How about a bit more work around the farm and less movie making?

BILLIE: Movie making? Whatever.

PRU: God, I hate that word.

MAXINE: (*to JEREMIAH*) Wrap up the food, would you?

BILLIE: You don't get it. It's great content. People younger than you guys respect it.

PRU: You're right. I don't get it.

BILLIE: (*reading from her phone*)   I'm getting comments! "Sick American Gothic vibe." See?

JEREMIAH: Sick?

BILLIE: 'Sick' is good.

DUANE: 'Sick' is really good.

PRU: (*eating a sandwich*) How would you know?

DUANE: I know things.

BILLIE: (*looking out the window*) The sky is friggin' green! Oh, man, I've got to get this.

BILLIE runs outside.

PRU: (*to BILLIE*) Billie, get back in here.

PRU: (*to JEREMIAH*) Go get her. She's going to get drenched.

MAXINE: (*grabbing an umbrella*) I'll go.

PRU: No, Mom.

JEREMIAH is having a hard time with the plastic wrap to cover the sandwiches.

MAXINE: Hon, I've got this. Help your husband.

JEREMIAH: (*to PRU*) What did you want to tell me?

DUANE's ears perk up. PRU and JEREMIAH step further away from DUANE. DUANE sips his beer but he is all ears.

PRU: Duane, do you mind? This is private.

DUANE: (*stays at the counter*) I'm half deaf.

PRU: It's the other half I'm worried about.

PRU gets closer to JEREMIAH.

PRU: We got an offer on the farm.

JEREMIAH: What's gotten into you?

PRU: It's a good offer.

JEREMIAH: Why would you even consider it?

PRU: It's more than what the Andersons got for their farm. They're demanding an answer by next week.

JEREMIAH shakes his head.

PRU: It's a good time to sell.

JEREMIAH: And do what, Pru? What will we do instead?

PRU: Oh, I don't know. Maybe be happy?

JEREMIAH: Happy?

MAXINE and BILLIE come back inside.

BILLIE: That was awesome.

PRU: Get a towel, you're dripping all over the place.

MAXINE: *(throwing BILLIE a dishtowel)* All this food. What a waste.

A very loud tornado warning siren sounds.

PRU: Oh, my God.

MAXINE: Everyone to the basement. Now!

The stage goes dark.

There is the sound of wind howling, and the footsteps of people rushing down the stairs. Then scary silence.

Camping lights illuminate MAXINE, DUANE, BILLIE, JEREMIAH and PRU huddled together on the floor, as if they have gone down the stairs to the dank basement. All are church quiet.

BILLIE: My ears popped.

MAXINE: Mine, too.

PRU: Why can't we hear anything?

JEREMIAH: Maybe it's a good thing?

BILLIE: Like we won't get hit?

MAXINE: Or we might be right in the center of it, the chaos and fury circling around us.

PRU: Oh, that helps, Mom.

MAXINE: What? We wait. We pray.

PRU: They're happening more often, the tornadoes. And stronger. Not just Nebraska.

JEREMIAH: Maybe now's not the best time to talk about climate change.

PRU: Just saying.

MAXINE: There's nothing we can do.

BILLIE: *(begins pacing anxiously)* Moving to another state might be a good option, like California.

PRU: You only have to worry about earthquakes and wildfires there.

DUANE: And hippies.

PRU: *(laughing)*   Hippies.

The sound of the wind intensifies. They hear muffled sounds of things hitting the walls of the diner. JEREMIAH surreptitiously takes a sip from his flask.

BILLIE: I can't breathe. There's no air in here.

PRU: *(to JEREMIAH)* Seriously?

JEREMIAH: What?

PRU: It's not even noon.

DUANE: It's noon somewhere.

JEREMIAH laughs. PRU scowls at DUANE.

JEREMIAH: *(to PRU)* Want some?

PRU: No, I don't want some.

JEREMIAH puts away the flask.

BILLIE: Can I have a sip?

PRU: No, you may not.

BILLIE: I'm almost 19.

PRU: You just turned 18.

BILLIE: This could be my last opportunity.

MAXINE: Billie! Don't even joke about that.

BILLIE: What, Gram? This could be it, right? RIGHT?

DUANE: Don't you worry, hon. We'll be OK.

BILLIE: How do you know? How does anybody know?

JEREMIAH takes another swig from the flask.

JEREMIAH: *(to BILLIE)* You shouldn't drink if you have long Covid.

PRU: Screw it. Just party on. Who cares what I think?

Another loud sound from outside, maybe a tree falling.

BILLIE: *(visibly scared, crying, shaking)* Oh God, oh God, oh God.

PRU: *(putting her arms around BILLIE)* It's OK, love.

BILLIE gets up.

BILLIE: *(in full panic mode)* Where's my phone? Oh my God, it's upstairs. I've got to get it.

BILLIE heads to the stairs.

PRU AND MAXINE: Billie, no!

BILLIE: My whole fucking life is on that phone!

PRU grabs BILLIE and holds her tight. DUANE runs upstairs.

MAXINE: No, Duane. Don't—

DUANE runs up the stairs. The wind howls as they wait for him to return.

A loud bang is heard outside. It becomes very quiet.

PRU: *(to JEREMIAH)* Why did you let him go up there? He could get killed.

JEREMIAH: I didn't "let" him.

PRU: And yet...

MAXINE: Stop it, you two.

A moment passes then DUANE returns with the phone and a fresh beer. He hands the phone to BILLIE.

BILLIE: *(grabbing her phone)* Thank you!

DUANE cracks open his beer can and sits beside MAXINE. BILLIE sits next to PRU.

MAXINE: *(looking gratefully at DUANE)* You're a damn fool... A damn fool.

They all sit without speaking while the muffled loud sounds from outside continue.

DUANE: So, a moth goes to see a podiatrist. He's been having the worst time of his whole life. His wife has left him for the guy who sells honey at the local farmer's market. A young guy with a nice smile. Like the Carson boy, remember him? Moved to California, I think. And the moth's kids, oh man, it's just heartbreaking what happened—

The all-clear siren interrupts DUANE. The wind dies down. It's quiet.

A rooster crows.

MAXINE: I'm going up.

JEREMIAH: Are you sure it's safe? Let's wait.

MAXINE: You heard him. Cock-a-doodle-do.

SCENE 2

Later that day.

MAXINE is in the diner. Some of the windows are broken, furniture is toppled but the diner is still standing. Leaves and glass are scattered around the floor. MAXINE is sweeping and picking up debris. DUANE enters.

DUANE: None of the power lines are down on Main Street.

MAXINE: That's good. Thanks for checking.

DUANE: Let me help you with that.

DUANE picks up some chairs from the floor.

DUANE: Where is everyone else?

MAXINE: Pru and the family went back to check on our houses.

DUANE: Is everything OK?

MAXINE: Yeah, it looks like it. Pru called. She said we were lucky.

DUANE: Damn lucky. The Carson's barn is gone. And two of their cows are nowhere to be found.

MAXINE: Two?

DUANE: Yeah.

MAXINE: What a shame. Remember the last one in '98?

DUANE: Who could forget? I noticed the City Limit sign blew away.

MAXINE: Then you haven't been paying much attention. That's been gone a while now.

DUANE: You sure?

MAXINE: I'm the mayor, remember?

DUANE: Right. And the tax collector, and the librarian and—

MAXINE: Alright! Anyway, we should get a new sign. The one that blew away was out of date anyway. It's on my list.

MAXINE looks out the window.

MAXINE: The church survived.

DUANE: Not much left to take down since our last big storm.

MAXINE: Did you know my father built that church? Before that we use to go over to St. Matthew's in Aurora. It was nice and all but my Dad figured that Possum Trot deserved its own church. Mind you, there was no priest or nothing. My Dad just figured if you built a church, one would come.

DUANE: 'Field of Dreams?'

MAXINE: I love Kevin Costner!

DUANE: What a great movie.

MAXINE: He got the Carson brothers, my uncle Bob and some other folks and they built it. My mother found a picture in a book of Norwegian churches. The window was rescued from the Catholic school that burned down in '31. And after the railroad came, the church was full every Sunday.

DUANE: I went there a few times. The acoustics were pretty good, for a church.

MAXINE: (*smiling*) Right.

DUANE: (*nervously*): I was thinking, it's a crazy idea but how about you and me—

MAXINE: —A lot of memories. You and Mary got married there, right?

DUANE: We sure did. Hell, everybody got hitched there.

MAXINE: I'm sorry, what were you going to say?

DUANE: I was wondering if—

MAXINE: —Oh, my heavens. Look at that.

MAXINE gets up and goes to a table that is lying on its side.

MAXINE: LH + ML. I carved that when I was a girl.

DUANE: I remember that girl. I had such a crush.

MAXINE: You did not.

DUANE: Then along came Larry.

BILLIE who has been standing near the front door, watching MAXINE and DUANE, enters the diner.

MAXINE: Hello, sweetheart.

BILLIE: I was looking for Duane. I saw his truck outside.

DUANE: Hi, kiddo. What's up?

MAXINE: I'm going to tackle the kitchen.

MAXINE kisses BILLIE's head and pats DUANE's shoulder and leaves. DUANE watches her leave the dining room.

BILLIE: Look at you! You still have a crush!

DUANE: Eavesdropping again?

BILLIE: Can you take me to Aurora?

DUANE: Right now?

BILLIE: Yeah.

DUANE: I just got here. Can it wait?

BILLIE: Not really.

DUANE: You want me to drive you there now, bring you back here and then go home again after the card game?

BILLIE: I wouldn't ask if it wasn't important.

DUANE: And where in particular are we going?

BILLIE: Walmart.

DUANE: Walmart? Alright.

BILLIE: Thanks.

DUANE: You're lucky I like you.

DUANE gets up and starts walking out.

DUANE: Do you know where Walmart keeps the Terminator toys?

BILLIE: Where?

DUANE: Aisle B, back.

BILLIE forces a laugh.

DUANE: *(cont.)* That's it?

BILLIE: I give it a three, but your accent kind of sucks, no offence.

DUANE: None taken.

DUANE and BILLIE put some tables and chairs right-side up.

DUANE: Your Gram and I were just talking and it made me wonder. Remind me, do you know anything about your granddad?

BILLIE: Not really. Did you know him?

DUANE: We were neighbors until my folks moved us to Aurora.

BILLIE: What was he like?

DUANE: Everybody liked him. He was one of those guys who treated a jughead like me like I was something. He was a good guy.

BILLIE picks up her phone, points it at DUANE.

BILLIE: Tell me a story about him.

DUANE: Why do you video tape everything?

BILLIE: Why do you hang around my Gram so much?

DUANE: *(sheepishly)* I don't know.

BILLIE: Come on, story time.

DUANE: Yeah, I guess I can tell you a story. Your Gramps played the guitar, did you know that? He was good. When we were 16, we decided to form a band. I played the keyboard. We were going to be the next Allman Brothers. Ever hear of them?

BILLIE: Are you kidding me? Midnight Rider? Epic.

DUANE : It was me, your Granddad and Rusty. We called ourselves The Trots.

BILLIE: The Trots? That's sick!

DUANE: We would practice at the church on Saturday afternoons in exchange for playing at the Sunday Folk Mass.

BILLIE: Groupies must have been a big problem.

DUANE: Yeah, well, Larry, your Gramps, did have a girl he was sweet on. In fact, we were going to play at her birthday party. Our first big gig. He wrote her a song. A surprisingly good love song. Well, that Saturday I came in early to our rehearsal. Nobody else was there. I started playing that song and who should come into the church to do the Sunday flowers but the birthday girl. She sat quietly in the back. I didn't even know she was there until I finished. She came up to me with tears in her eyes and said that that was the prettiest song she had ever heard. She asked me who wrote it, and me, joking around, said that I did. The way she looked at me knocked the sense right out of me. That night at her party Larry introduced the song, saying that he wrote it especially for the birthday girl. Afterwards, when Larry went up to her, expecting a kiss or at least some sweet words of thanks, she called him a liar right to his face. Pointing at me, she said "I know that Duane wrote that song. I heard him practicing at the church. He told me he wrote it." I stuttered a denial, an explanation, but that didn't stop Larry from turning around and punching me in the gut.

BILLIE: Ouch. What happened? Did you ever see her again.

DUANE: Your Gramps married her. And the band broke up.

BILLIE: Good story.

DUANE: Tell me why are we going to Walmart? Is Amazon closed?

BILLIE: I need to get something, that's all. Didn't want to wait.

DUANE: Everything OK? You got another weird disease?

BILLIE: I really want to hear that birthday song.

DUANE: Yeah, that's not gonna happen.

BILLIE: Can we go now?

DUANE: Yeah. Let's go.

SCENE 3

It is late afternoon in the diner. PRU is putting up decorations for the party. The radio is on, country music playing. The room is filled with streamers and balloons and a gold banner that says 'Happy 50th Anniversary.' It originally said 'Happy 50th Wedding Anniversary' but Pru cut out the Wedding part.

MAXINE enters the diner carrying bags of food.

MAXINE: How can we still have this party? It don't feel right.

PRU: Everyone needs this party. It will take our minds off stuff.

MAXINE: Like tornadoes?

PRU: Yeah, stuff like that.

MAXINE: Is Billie back yet? She usually helps me set up the card game.

PRU: I'll help. Not sure what's going on with that girl. You know, she and Tyler broke up. She won't tell me details—

MAXINE: —Who?

PRU: Tyler? The boy from Lincoln? They met at 4H Club?

MAXINE: Oh, right. The ballplayer.

PRU: He got accepted to Omaha. Full scholarship.

MAXINE: I actually liked him. He wasn't a complete idiot.

PRU: Spoken like a true Christian.

MAXINE: He used full sentences and looked you in the eye.

MAXINE puts away the food delivery, washes some glasses, wipes down tables, and grabs some chairs for the card game.

MAXINE: Come on, grab some chairs.

PRU: Can I ask you something?

MAXINE: Go on.

PRU: Uh...

MAXINE: What already?

PRU: Do you ever think about closing the diner?

MAXINE: Why would I do that?

PRU: It's a lot for you to handle.

MAXINE: I'm doing just fine, thank you very much.

PRU: But, you know, you're—

MAXINE: I'm what? And choose your words carefully.

PRU: You're getting on.

MAXINE: I figure when I die, just lock the door and turn out the light.

PRU: That's dark, Mom. You could sell the place and travel—

MAXINE: Why would I do that?

PRU: Because you can.

MAXINE: Just put a sign on the door—Gone Fishing?

PRU: You used to talk about going to see the Grand Canyon.

MAXINE: That was your Dad. How could I leave this place? What would folks do without us?

PRU: They'd survive.

MAXINE: (*laughing*) I wouldn't.

PRU: Sure, you would. The place needs work, Mom. A lot of work.

MAXINE: It just needs a little fixing up. I'll get some new tables, some paint.

PRU: It needs more than that. You have an outhouse, for God's sake.

MAXINE: You could buy it. I'll give you a good price.

PRU: I can't run a diner. I'm a terrible cook. Jeremiah does most of the cooking.

MAXINE: Don't worry, I'm joking.

PRU: Right.

MAXINE: And you are a terrible cook.

PRU: Thanks.

MAXINE: But your coconut cakes are surprisingly delicious.

PRU starts laughing.

MAXINE: What's so funny?

PRU shakes her head.

MAXINE: What?

PRU: I get them at Costco.

MAXINE: You do not!

PRU: I do. I buy them in bulk and put them in the big freezer in our garage. Anyway, you can't just serve coconut cake.

MAXINE: Add hot coffee and cold beer and you're set. This place isn't about the food.

PRU: Does this place break even?

MAXINE: What? No, don't you, don't—

JEREMIAH: (*entering the diner*)—Don't what?

MAXINE: Nothing. I'm going to grab a sweater.

MAXINE leaves the diner.

JEREMIAH: What was that all about?

PRU: What is she going to do, run this place until she drops?

JEREMIAH: Probably.

PRU: I know her back is acting up again. She thinks I don't notice her limping. And have you noticed the vegetable garden? It's a complete jungle out there. Dad loved his garden.

JEREMIAH: (*grabbing a beer*) She's gonna outlive us all.

PRU: What did the bank say?

JEREMIAH: Nothing good.

PRU: What exactly did they say?

JEREMIAH: They won't give us another line of credit. Losing the sorghum crop didn't help. I'll sort it out.

PRU: The writing is on the wall. Why can't you see it? Am I the only one?

JEREMIAH: No, it isn't. We've had rough patches before. We will get through this.

PRU: I don't want to get through this. You're not sleeping. You've been biting your lip again.

JEREMIAH: Have I?

JEREMIAH moves his lips around.

PRU: You're drinking more.

JEREMIAH: *(putting the beer down)* You counting my beers now?

PRU: I'm just worried.

PRU puts her hand on his shoulder, he gets up abruptly and walks away from her.

JEREMIAH: Don't be. I was thinking we should plant some soybeans. That's easier on the soil. And the prices are good right now.

PRU: We can't afford a new crop.

JEREMIAH: You don't know that!

PRU: Jeez, what's with the tone?

JEREMIAH: There's no tone.

PRU: There's definitely a tone. Aren't you tired of worrying about the price of corn or soybeans? Droughts? Floods? Tornadoes? Broken machinery that we can't afford to fix? Haven't you had enough?

JEREMIAH: My Dad trusted me to take care of the farm. If I can't keep that promise, what does that say about me?

PRU: He'd understand. It's a lot harder now. We aren't competing with other family farms any more. It's not the same.

JEREMIAH: It will be alright.

PRU: At what cost? There's no shame in walking away and changing course.

JEREMIAH: Walking away? Are you telling me that you want to leave our life here, everything that we built together? Everything our parents and their parents built.

PRU: You're not hearing me.

JEREMIAH: That's what it sounds like to me.

PRU: I'm not saying that.

JEREMIAH: Or are you telling me that you want to leave me? You're not happy. If that's it, just say it.

PRU: No, that's not what I meant at all. Maybe we make a change together. If we sold the land, we could buy a little place in Omaha or Aurora. We could take one of those cruises down the Mississippi.

JEREMIAH: Don't you get it? I like it here. I have purpose. I like walking through the front door of the house that my Dad made, creaky doors and all. I like playing poker with our friends. Even if they cheat like Duane, wearing those sunglasses to hide his twitching eye when he has a good hand. I like helping out here with your Mom when I can. I like knowing the roads like the back of my hand. The mailman waves when he goes by in his truck. It makes me feel like I'm part of something, part of somewhere. I didn't have that when I was growing up.

PRU: I know.

JEREMIAH: Four different homes before I was 15. You know that. Don't ask me to start over again.

PRU: Can't you even think about what I'm saying, what I'm feeling?

MAXINE enters the diner.

MAXINE: Who's up for a game tonight?

JEREMIAH: I am.

MAXINE: Feeling lucky this week, Pru?

PRU: You guys play without me.

MAXINE: Why would we do that?

JEREMIAH: It's Thursday. It's poker night.

PRU: *(to Jeremiah)* And that's what we do on Thursdays.

MAXINE: *(to Pru)* What's eating at you?

PRU: Nothing. I'm tired, that's all.

MAXINE: We can't play poker with just two.

JEREMIAH: Come on, don't spoil it for everyone.

PRU: *(to Jeremiah)* That's not fair.

JEREMIAH: You know what I meant.

PRU: Yeah, I know what you meant.

JEREMIAH: We need you.

MAXINE: And your money! How about a beer?

JEREMIAH: *(to Maxine)* Yeah.

MAXINE: I was talking to her.

DUANE enters.

DUANE: Hey.

DUANE notices all the decorations.

DUANE: Pretty fancy for a card game.

PRU: It's for the party.

DUANE: I know, sweetheart. It looks nice.

JEREMIAH: *(handing her the beer from Maxine)* Please.

PRU takes the beer, standing away from the table.

DUANE: Sit yourself down, Pru. You're my lucky charm.

JEREMIAH: *(pats the chair next to him)* Yeah, sit.

PRU ignores JEREMIAH and sits across from him.

JEREMIAH: Where's Billie? Wasn't she with you today?

DUANE: She'll be here in a minute. She had to make a pit stop.

JEREMIAH: What are we playing tonight? Texas Hold'em?

MAXINE: Is that the one with the cards in the middle of the table?

PRU: Who are you kidding, Mom? You won this diner in a poker game.

MAXINE: No, I did not. That's a local myth.

JEREMIAH: Anyone else coming tonight?

MAXINE: I don't think so. Most folks are coming in tomorrow for the party.

BILLIE enters and sits at the table with the others. She seems preoccupied.

PRU: You OK, hon?

MAXINE: Want something to eat?

BILLIE: No, Gram. I'm alright.

JEREMIAH: *(to Billie)* You playing?

BILLIE: Yeah, I guess.

JEREMIAH: *(dealing cards)* OK then. Let's play.

Everyone puts some change on the table. JERMIAH deals two cards to each player.

PRU: A nickel.

MAXINE: Same.

DUANE: Yep.

BILLIE is staring at her phone.

JEREMIAH: Billie, what are you doing?

BILLIE: Nothing.

JEREMIAH: Are you in or out?

BILLIE: I fold.

MAXINE: *(looking at Billie's cards)* Why did you do that, child? Never fold with just your hole cards.

BILLIE: It doesn't matter.

MAXINE: You're giving up before the game even starts.

BILLIE shrugs. JEREMIAH puts down three cards in the center of the table, face down.

MAXINE: *(to Jeremiah)* Who folds on the first hand, that's all I'm saying.

PRU: Mom, please.

MAXINE: What?

PRU: It's just a card game.

MAXINE shows BILLIE her cards.

MAXINE: I had nothing in the beginning but look. See what happened?

BILLIE: *(upset)* Oh, my God. I know how to play.

BILLIE leaves the diner.

PRU: Really, Mom?

MAXINE: What did I do?

PRU: You can be a little judgey.

MAXINE: I didn't mean to upset her.

PRU: Yet you did.

MAXINE: Should I go out there?

PRU: Let her be.

DUANE: Don't worry, Max.

MAXINE: She's usually a sharp card player.

DUANE: I don't think it's the card game.

JEREMIAH: You took her to Aurora today, right?

DUANE: Yeah, I did.

MAXINE: Where did you guys go?

PRU: Did something upset her today?

DUANE: We went to Walmart.

BILLIE runs back into the diner.

BILLIE: *(Shaken)* You gotta come!

PRU: What is it?

BILLIE: *(trying to catch her breath)* Outside.

MAXINE: Calm down, child.

BILLIE: In the back. On the roof.

JEREMIAH: Someone is on the roof?

BILLIE: Go outside.

DUANE: Is it that white owl?

BILLIE: It's not an owl.

DUANE: One of those drone things?

BILLIE: No!

MAXINE: Oh, good lord, what the hell is it?

BILLIE: There's a cow on the roof.

JEREMIAH: Holy Shit! A cow? Like... a whole cow?

BILLIE: A fucking cow!

MAXINE: Did she say cow?

PRU: A fucking cow.

MAXINE: I don't understand.

PRU: Are you on drugs?

BILLIE: There is a whole cow on the frigging roof.

PRU: Can you tell if it's dead or alive?

MAXINE: How did a cow get on my roof?

BILLIE: *(exasperated)* Oh my God, people.

> *BILLIE and the others go outside to look at the cow on the roof under a star-lit night sky.*

SCENE 4

Moments later, MAXINE, PRU, JEREMIAH and DUANE come into the diner.

DUANE: I saw a "C" branded on his backside. Should we let the Carsons know?

PRU: Is it their responsibility to get it down from the roof?

JEREMIAH: It's not their fault she's up there—

PRU: I'm not blaming them. I'm just saying—

JEREMIAH: —Blame mother nature, if you're going to blame anyone.

PRU: It's their goddamned cow.

MAXINE: Is she definitely dead?

BILLIE enters, carrying her phone.

BILLIE: She's tangled up in some branches. She must have hit the big oak first and then fell. She flew what? A couple of miles? She must have been scared shitless.

MAXINE frowns at BILLIE.

BILLIE: Sorry.

MAXINE: We don't know for sure if the cow is dead or not.

BILLIE: She's not moving.

DUANE: Or moo-ing.

PRU: Come on, after all that, she's must be dead.

DUANE: She's gotta weigh at least 1,400 pounds.

MAXINE: 1,400 pounds? Can my roof hold that?

DUANE: Not for long.

MAXINE: Don't just stand there. We've got to do something.

DUANE: Not much we can do right now.

JEREMIAH: We can't just push her off the roof. It's not like a big dead squirrel.

PRU: It's a miracle that it didn't slam right through the roof.

JEREMIAH: We need a crane.

PRU: Where do we find a crane?

JEREMIAH: Maybe someone in Aurora? We need to wait until morning.

MAXINE: We just stand here and wait?

BILLIE: Maybe wait over here?

BILLIE points to the area in the diner the farthest away from the kitchen. DUANE leaves the diner, taking out his phone as he walks out.

PRU: We can call first thing in the morning before the party.

MAXINE: The party? Oh, dear lord.

BILLIE: Old Bessie is going to start smelling pretty rank by tomorrow.

JEREMIAH: We should probably call off the party.

BILLIE: *(pointing to the ceiling)* We have a ticking time bomb situation.

Duane comes back in.

DUANE: I got hold of my buddy at the Aurora Police station. They've got one crane, technically part of Aurora Utilities—

JEREMIAH: —Great.

DUANE: —But there are lots of utility poles down so the earliest he could get the crane here is maybe three days.

JEREMIAH: I'll figure it out, OK?

MAXINE: Three days? That won't work.

JEREMIAH: Don't worry. I'll fix it.

PRU: I should send out an email, letting everyone know that the party has been cancelled.

BILLIE: Where's the ladder?

MAXINE: Why on earth do you want a ladder?

BILLIE: I want to film this. I mean, it's pretty awesome.

DUANE: Are you crazy? You should definitely not be doing anything stupid like climbing a ladder now.

BILLIE: How else am I going to film the cow?

DUANE: *(to BILLIE)* Don't you think it's way too dangerous?

BILLIE: *(getting angry)* I'm fine!

PRU: Billie climbs like a mountain goat. Why are you so worried?

DUANE: I'm not worried.

PRU: What's going on?

BILLIE: Nothing's going on. I want to film the cow, that's all.

PRU: No, something's up. I can feel it. You've been acting strangely since you got back from Aurora. Did something happen there? Is this about Tyler?

BILLIE: No. Duane took me to Walmart. End of story.

PRU: What did you need at Walmart?

BILLIE: I'd rather not say. It's kind of private.

PRU: Private? So, you went with Duane here, our town crier?

BILLIE: Yeah.

PRU: Come on.

BILLIE gets a ladder from behind the counter.

BILLIE: Drop it, OK? Nothing happened. I'm fine.

DUANE: Don't let her go up that ladder. It's not safe. She and the cow could both come tumbling down.

MAXINE: Out with it, Duane.

JEREMIAH: What aren't you telling us?

DUANE: It's none of my business.

JEREMIAH: His eye is twitching. Do you see it?

MAXINE: I sure do.

BILLIE: Leave him alone.

DUANE: Hey, she's your kid. If you're not worried, why should I be? What do I know? I'm gonna hit the road.

PRU: No, mister, sit yourself down.

BILLIE: Let him be.

BILLIE: (*to DUANE*) You don't have to go.

DUANE: (*to BILLIE*) I didn't mean to—

BILLIE: (*to DUANE*)—It's OK. I needed a pregnancy test.

PRU: Oh, dear Lord.

A slight sound is heard coming from the roof.

MAXINE: Oh, my God. Did you hear that?

DUANE: It could just be a branch.

JEREMIAH: (*to PRU*) What?

DUANE: I said that it could just be a branch.

JEREMIAH: (*pointing to BILLIE*) No, not you. Her.

PRU: She said she needed a pregnancy test.

JEREMIAH: That's what I thought she said. Oh, Billie—

MAXINE: —It's not enough that there's a cow on the roof.

PRU: And?

BILLIE: And I'm pregnant.

PRU: Oh, Billie.

PRU paces, JEREMIAH broods, MAXINE sits down, BILLIE leaves.

DUANE: A cow on the roof and a bun in the oven. Anyone else want a beer?

EVERYONE: No!

SCENE 5

Diner, later that night. MAXINE is by herself, clearing away the beer cans. She takes the photo of her late husband and brings it to a table, far from the kitchen.

MAXINE: *(to the photo)* You sure are missing all the fun. Never a dull moment.

MAXINE goes to a cupboard and takes out a bottle of bourbon and pours herself a glass. She raises her glass to her husband's photo.

MAXINE: To you, my love.

She takes a drink.

MAXINE: Remember when we first bought the diner? Your Dad didn't speak to me for months. He blamed me for stealing you away from the family farm. But after he sold that place, we couldn't get him to leave, like he was holding court here at that corner table. Sometimes this felt more like a social club. More talking than eating.

MAXINE walks to the window and looks out.

MAXINE: Pru thinks I should sell the place and go traveling. We used to talk about that, remember? At night, with my head on your chest, listing all the places we would go to—New York, Hollywood, Branson, Missouri. How we would eat like kings and see the sights. And then you'd wrap your arms around me and I'd fall asleep listening to the crickets, wanting to be nowhere but here.

MAXINE tries to rehang one of the decorations that has fallen during all the commotion. She pulls a muscle and winces in pain.

MAXINE: Big party tomorrow celebrating 50 years of running this joint. Pru's idea. But with the tornado, the road closed and the cow on the roof, who knows? Could be a pretty small celebration. We used to have some grand parties here.

Remember the big to-do we had for the Mitchell's? Who says cattle struck by lightning doesn't taste good?

She pours herself another shot of bourbon.

MAXINE: Funny thing. I miss the train whistle. Late at night, I'd hear it and my mind would wander. I'd imagine where it came from, where was it going. It was like we were connected to something bigger than Possum Trot. We were part of the Northern Line.

She takes a sip of the bourbon.

MAXINE: It's not just the train whistle, I miss the church bells. I miss dogs barking. I miss the sound of kids playing. I even miss your snoring.

She is silent for a moment.

MAXINE: Ah, hell, I miss noise! There's hardly anyone left. Some sold their farms, businesses closed up, kids moved away and some just couldn't take it anymore. Like Burt and Bob Putnam. Breaks your heart.

She hears a creaking noise coming from the kitchen. Not a big noise, just something a bit worrisome. The beer sign flickers off. She goes to tap it but it doesn't turn back on. She tries again. No luck.

MAXINE: *(rubbing her injured back)* I should leave. Disaster is looming.

JEREMIAH enters the diner.

JEREMIAH: I saw the light on.

MAXINE: Just closing up.

JEREMIAH: You, OK?

MAXINE: Peachy. You?

JEREMIAH: Oh, yeah, peachy.

MAXINE: *(holding the bottle)* Want a quick one? You're risking your life being in here, you know?

JEREMIAH nods his head. She pours a glass and hands it to him.

JEREMIAH: *(noticing the photo)* To Larry!

MAXINE: *(smiling)* To Larry.

MAXINE: Are Pru and Billie at home?

JEREMIAH: Yeah.

MAXINE: What a day, huh?

JEREMIAH: Yeah. *(Pause)* Max, do you think times are harder now, for farming, I mean?

MAXINE: It's never been easy. You're married to the land and to whatever nature throws at you.

JEREMIAH: I mean, compared to when you opened this place.

MAXINE: The farms were smaller. You knew your neighbors. But the hours are the same—long. The work is hard. Nature is pretty unforgiving.

JEREMIAH: My Dad did alright. He provided for us. We never went without the basics. And he seemed happy.

MAXINE: I liked your Dad. He was a good man.

JEREMIAH: Yeah, he was.

MAXINE: It's not for everybody.

JEREMIAH: No, it's not.

MAXINE: It's hard, hon.

JEREMIAH: Yeah.

JEREMIAH throws back the rest of his drink and pours himself another shot of bourbon.

MAXINE: What's going on? Are you alright?

JEREMIAH: The last time I was in Omaha I saw this bumper sticker. It said "Tradition is peer pressure from dead people."

MAXINE: Dead people? You talking about ghosts?

JEREMIAH: No, not ghosts. Uh, more like ancestors, you know.

MAXINE: OK.

JEREMIAH: Do you think it's true?

MAXINE: I don't know. Traditions are important... common beliefs... community. It makes us feel part of something bigger than ourselves. But what do I know, the world's changing.

JEREMIAH: It's confining, though, isn't it? To fit in?

MAXINE: But I think we have a choice.

JEREMIAH: Do we really?

MAXINE: To a certain extent, yes.

JEREMIAH : I don't feel like I have a choice.

MAXINE: You're too young to know this but the guy who owned this diner before us was famous for his Sunday fried chicken. Folks would wait in line for it. He raised the chickens, he cut their heads off, he fried them in lard. We took over and no more fried chicken. Nothing's going to get me to chop off chicken heads. Now it's microwaved nuggets. Tradition be damned.

JEREMIAH: No, no, it's not about recipes. You don't understand. You don't get it.

MAXINE: I'm trying.

JEREMIAH: I've given it my all, you know? I really have. Year after year. For Pru, for Billie. For my Dad. But, no matter what I do, it's not enough.

MAXINE: You've done your best.

JEREMIAH: Exactly. And look at me, Max.

MAXINE: Let me ask you this. Do you like farming?

JEREMIAH: Does it matter?

MAXINE: Maybe what you're feeling is just guilt? Or maybe it's as simple as you're not doing what you want to do.

JEREMIAH: It's what I am supposed to do. That's the point. And I suck at it. Don't you see?

MAXINE: I was supposed to be a farmer's wife.

JEREMIAH: It's not the same.

MAXINE: Isn't it?

JEREMIAH starts to pour himself another drink.

MAXINE: I think it's time for you to go home and get some sleep so you can take care of our little situation here *(pointing to the roof.)*

JEREMIAH: *(looking up)* Yeah.

JEREMIAH gets up and goes to the door and looks back at MAXINE.

JEREMIAH: Thanks, Max. For everything.

JEREMIAH takes a long look around the diner then leaves.

MAXINE puts the bottle of whiskey away and turns out the lights.

SCENE 6

Next morning at the diner. MAXINE is making coffee. BILLIE enters.

BILLIE: Morning, Gram.

MAXINE: Stay over here.

BILLIE: *(moving to a safer location)* How's Bessie?

MAXINE: Making me a nervous wreck.

BILLIE: I get it.

MAXINE: Hungry?

BILLIE: Oh, yeah, I could eat.

MAXINE: Stale donut?

BILLIE: Sounds good.

MAXINE: *(taking the donut from the counter display)* I don't want to go in the danger zone.

BILLIE: No, I hear ya.

MAXINE: How are you?

BILLIE: Ah, you know.

MAXINE: Did you tell the father yet?

BILLIE: No.

MAXINE: I'm assuming Taylor?

BILLIE: Tyler.

MAXINE: You're going to tell him soon?

BILLIE: I don't know. The asshole broke up with me.

MAXINE frowns at the swearing.

BILLE: I can't have a baby.

MAXINE: You and Tyler can work this out.

BILLIE: He's already playing ball in Omaha. He's gone.

MAXINE: He can come back.

BILLIE: No, Gram. It's not just him. I want to bring something beautiful into the world someday, but right now, all I have are dreams. And those aren't enough to raise a baby. And...

MAXINE: And what?

BILLIE: I got into college. A great art college. Cal Arts in California.

MAXINE: What?

BILLIE: I was going to tell you guys at the party.

MAXINE: I didn't know that you applied to any colleges.

BILLIE: No one did. I didn't think I had a chance of getting in but I did.

MAXINE: That's wonderful. I'm so proud of you.

BILLIE: Yeah, well, I screwed it all up.

MAXINE: You're quite certain you're pregnant?

BILLIE: I peed on a stick.

MAXINE: It could be a false positive. You should test again.

BILLIE: Gram, what am I going to do?

MAXINE: There are options.

BILLIE: Not here, not in this state. God, I was so stupid. What a mess.

BILLIE shakes her head and begins to cry.

BILLIE: Shit.

MAXINE puts her arms around BILLIE.

MAXINE: Art school, huh? That's what you want to do—be an artist?

BILLIE: It's the only thing I'm kind of good at.

MAXINE: You can see some of your early work over there carved into the corner table.

BILLIE: Oh, my God, it's still there?

MAXINE: You dug deep.

BILLIE: It's a portrait of Dad.

MAXINE: I thought it was a smiley face.

> *BILLIE's phone rings.*

BILLIE: It's Tyler. I'm gonna take this outside.

> *BILLIE leaves the diner.*

> *DUANE enters carrying a case of beer. You can hear the sound of something dripping in the kitchen.*

MAXINE: What the hell is that now?

DUANE: Morning, Max.

MAXINE: *(distracted by the sound)* Hey.

DUANE: Where do you want this?

MAXINE: *(looking up at the ceiling)* Normally I'd say the kitchen. Do you hear that?

DUANE: *(putting it on the counter)* Here looks good. Hear what?

MAXINE: That dripping sound.

> *DUANE heads to the kitchen to investigate the sound.*

MAXINE: Don't go in there!

DUANE: I was checking out the sound—

MAXINE: Leave it.

DUANE: OK. I called about the crane again. Could be tomorrow.

MAXINE: What time?

DUANE: I don't know.

MAXINE: This waiting is killing me. I mean, any minute, and boom!

DUANE: If you can't take the heat—

MAXINE:—Stay out of the kitchen. Goes without saying.

DUANE pours himself a cup of coffee but the pot is empty.

DUANE: No coffee today?

MAXINE: I just made it. A full pot.

DUANE: It's plugged in but it's not working. What kind of joint are you running here, lady?

MAXINE is struck by the comment.

DUANE: Hey, I'm kidding.

MAXINE: I'm running a joint that's falling apart.

DUANE gives her a hug.

DUANE: It's still my favorite joint. I'll check the outlet, OK?

MAXINE: You look way too chipper for someone who hasn't had any coffee yet.

DUANE: I've got some big news.

MAXINE: OK. And?

DUANE: I sold the feed store.

MAXINE: You did what?

DUANE: *(laughing)* Yep. They made me an offer I couldn't refuse—twice as much as I would make if I worked the rest of my life.

MAXINE: I don't know what to say.

DUANE: It's a good thing.

MAXINE: Yeah, it is...

DUANE: But?

MAXINE: But nothing. Congratulations.

DUANE: Come on, spill it.

MAXINE: It's another ending, that's all.

DUANE: It could be a new beginning.

MAXINE: How's that?

DUANE: Max, have you ever seen the sea?

MAXINE: Sure, I've seen the sea. I like nature shows.

DUANE: I mean feet in the sand, the ocean wind blowing your hair, the sound of seagulls, crashing waves seen the sea.

MAXINE: Does Lake Wanahoo count?

DUANE: Not a bit.

MAXINE: I took Pru there once to feed the ducks.

DUANE: I lived my whole life around here. And I've got no complaints. Mary and I had a good marriage, God rest her soul. But now, with the road ahead a lot shorter than the road behind me, there are some things I want to do before I die.

MAXINE: You have a bucket list?

DUANE: It's not really a list. I want to see the ocean.

MAXINE: Which one?

DUANE: It don't matter. We go east or west, we will end up at the sea.

MAXINE: We?

DUANE: I was hoping.

MAXINE: You want to leave?

DUANE: With you, Max.

MAXINE takes that in for a moment.

DUANE: Together.

MAXINE touches his hand.

DUANE: I was thinking of buying one of those RVs and we could hit the road.

(BEAT)

DUANE: Don't you want to experience what's out there?

MAXINE: Why does everyone ask me that? Pru just asked me if I want to visit the Grand Canyon. And then in you come with your big sea adventure. Do I look like I need a vacation?

DUANE: Don't think 'vacation,' think 'adventure.'

MAXINE: It's the same thing to me.

DUANE: What do you say?

MAXINE: It's sweet of you to ask.

DUANE: Just say that you'll think about it.

MAXINE: I'm the mayor.

DUANE: And you're doing a fine job. But are you happy?

MAXINE: I know it's silly but I take it seriously. I collect the taxes from myself to pay for the utilities here. Without me, there's no electricity, there's no water, there's no gas for the stove. There's no coffee in the morning and beer at night. These four walls are Possum Trot. The thought of turning off the lights one last time, closing that door and walking away from this place, these smoke-stained walls, grubby chairs and rickety tables seems unfathomable. I do that and this place is a ghost town. Like Billie said.

DUANE: That's a load of responsibility you're putting on yourself.

MAXINE: It's how I feel.

DUANE: Did you hear about the man who claimed he was responsible for the earthquake? He said it was all his fault.

MAXINE: *(tiny smile)* Oh, Lord. Why?

DUANE: I like to make you smile.

MAXINE: What's with all the sweet talk all of a sudden?

DUANE: What do you mean 'all of a sudden'? Maybe you haven't been listening till now.

MAXINE: I have but—

DUANE: But what?

MAXINE: I think that part of me is gone.

DUANE: Forever?

PRU enters the diner, agitated.

PRU: *(anxiously)* Have you seen Jeremiah?

MAXINE: And good morning to you.

PRU: Sorry. Morning. Jeremiah is missing.

MAXINE: What?

PRU: His truck is at the house but I can't find him. He's not answering his phone. I thought he'd be here.

MAXINE: Maybe he went to Aurora to see about the crane.

PRU: Without his truck?

MAXINE: Oh, right.

PRU: Duane, do you know anything?

DUANE: I haven't seen him since last night at the card game.

MAXINE: Maybe he's checking the fields?

PRU shakes her head. She calls him again. No answer.

MAXINE: When did you last see him?

PRU: Last night. I went to bed. He stayed up. He was drinking again. This morning when I woke up, he wasn't there. He hadn't come to bed.

MAXINE: He'll turn up.

PRU: *(angry)* How do you know that?

MAXINE: I'm sure there's nothing to worry about.

PRU: I have a bad feeling. He got all quiet-like.

MAXINE: He's never been a big talker.

PRU: We had a fight.

MAXINE: About what?

PRU: Selling the farm.

MAXINE: Really?

PRU: He's so stressed. And he got so mad at me. I'd never seen him like that.

MAXINE: He'll cool off.

PRU: What if he's done something stupid?

MAXINE: You think he ran away with some blonde cocktail waitress?

PRU: Of course not.

MAXINE: Then what?

PRU: What if... what if he...

MAXINE: Take a breath.

PRU: What if he's hurt himself?

MAXINE: The truck is still at home?

PRU: Yes.

MAXINE: OK, so he hasn't had a car accident.

PRU is getting very emotional.

PRU: Hurt himself like Burt or Bob Putnam hurt themselves.

MAXINE: No. He's not like that.

PRU: That's what we said when we heard about Burt and Bob.

MAXINE: Why would he do that?

PRU: We've lost a few crops. The bank won't refinance. The weather. Everything. Me.

DUANE: Maybe he fell asleep in the barn. Did you check there?

PRU: Of course, I did.

DUANE: He's probably getting something for the party.

MAXINE: Exactly. I gave him a long list.

PRU: Again, he doesn't have his truck.

MAXINE: Did you check the library?

PRU: The shed with Dad's old National Geographics? I'll check.

PRU leaves the diner, annoyed.

DUANE: *(to Maxine)* I'll take a look around.

MAXINE: I'm sorry.

DUANE: No, I understand, I do.

MAXINE: Thank you. Before you go, can we can throw a sheet over the cow?

DUANE: She's too big for that, I'm afraid.

MAXINE: At least cover the doorway here, in case she, uh, falls.

DUANE: Let me see what I can do.

DUANE gets a staple gun from a drawer and hangs the sheet from a wooden beam, as a privacy curtain between the cow in the kitchen and the rest of the diner.

PRU returns from the library.

PRU: He's not there.

BILLIE enters.

PRU: *(to Billie)* Do you know where your Dad is?

BILLIE: Isn't he at home?

PRU: *(loudly)* God, he's not at home!

BILLIE: Why are you yelling at me?

MAXINE: Your Mom is just worried, hon.

BILLIE: About what?

DUANE: We don't quite know where your Dad is.

PRU: Your Dad is missing. Something bad has happened. I can feel it.

BILLIE: But I saw his truck. He can't be far. Right?

MAXINE: Right. He can't be far. No need to worry.

BILLIE: Should we call the sheriff?

DUANE: It's too early for that. The person's gotta be missing for a day or so.

PRU: I'm going to walk around town.

BILLIE: I'll go with you.

PRU leaves the diner.

BILLIE: Mom, wait up.

BILLIE leaves.

MAXINE: *(to Duane)* He came in here late last night, after everybody had left. I didn't want to say anything to Pru but he was acting strange. Like there was definitely something worrying him.

DUANE: Like what?

MAXINE: He said that he's trying and it's hard. I think he was talking about taking care of the farm. And some bumper stick that he saw.

DUANE: Bumper sticker? What did it say?

MAXINE: Something about tradition and dead people.

DUANE: I saw one the other day that said 'Legalize Marinara.' Made me laugh.

MAXINE: —That's not the point, Duane.

DUANE: Right, of course.

MAXINE: He's not himself. That's all I'm saying.

SCENE 7

Later that day, PRU is sitting outside the diner, smoking a cigarette. BILLIE enters and sits next to her mom.

BILLIE: I thought you quit.

PRU: I did.

BILLIE: I bet he fell asleep somewhere.

PRU: Uh huh.

BILLIE: Or he locked himself in the hen house and can't get out.

PRU: Uh huh.

BILLIE: Did you look?

PRU: Did I look in the hen house? No, don't be daft.

BILLIE: Did you look in the truck? That would be a Dad move, sleeping in the truck.

PRU: Not there.

BILLIE: Are you mad at me?

PRU shakes her head.

BILLIE: It sure seems like it.

PRU: Jesus, Billie.

BILLIE: What?

PRU: Your dad is missing for one, the fucking cow, and you're...

BILLIE: What?

PRU: There's a lot going on.

BILLIE: I'm what?

PRU: Jesus, pregnant. I can't deal with that right now.

BILLIE: Sorry to burden you.

PRU: Is this for real or just a stunt to get your 'content'?

BILLIE: What the fuck! Are you kidding me? A stunt?

PRU: Your Dad is missing. Do you get that?

BILLIE: Yeah, I get that.

PRU: He is fucking missing.

BILLIE: Yes.

PRU: What were you thinking?

BILLIE: What do you want me to say? It was an accident.

PRU: An accident? You got yourself knocked-up. Give me a break.

BILLIE: I didn't plan it if that's what you're insinuating.

PRU: I don't get it. You don't tell me you were applying to college. And then you ask Duane to take you to Aurora? Why can't you come to me? I don't know what's going on with you.

BILLIE: You trying to make me feel worse? Because you're doing a really good job of it.

PRU: I thought you were smarter than this.

BILLIE: I can't believe you. You're my mom. Aren't you supposed to want to help? Isn't that your job?

PRU: Maybe Father Bob can help you.

BILLIE: Oh, that's great. Thanks. When all else fails, send me to a priest.

PRU: I don't know what to say to you.

BILLIE: That's helpful.
PRU: *(losing it)* What do you want from me?

BILLIE is silent.

PRU: What does Tyler say about all this?

BILLIE: He says it's up to me.

PRU: So? What's the plan? Get married? The two of you take over his Dad's little farm. Tell me.

BILLIE: I don't want to tell you anything when you're like this. I'll take care of it.

PRU: What does that mean? You'll take care of it.

BILLIE: I don't know.

PRU: You want to get rid of the baby?

BILLIE: God, I don't know. Yeah, maybe.

PRU: Christ almighty, I can't take anymore. I really can't.

BILLIE: I don't know what I'm going to do but can't you see how hard this is for me?

PRU: *(getting up to leave)* I wanted you to have a chance to be someone, someone other than me.

BILLIE: What does that mean? Do you hate your life?

PRU: No. But it was my choice. I loved your Dad.

PRU crushed by the past tense of her statement.

PRU: I love your Dad.

PRU cries. BILLIE hugs her.

SCENE 8

Late afternoon, time for the party. MAXINE and DUANE are in the diner. MAXINE drags in a large blue tarp from the storeroom.

MAXINE: I'll grab the ladder and you can toss this up on the roof.

DUANE: You limping?

MAXINE: No, I'm good.

MAXINE dumps the tarp on the floor, sits on a chair and sighs.

DUANE: That's for the rain, not a cow. No way in hell I can toss that on the roof by myself. 'A' for effort, though.

MAXINE: Well, with no crane in sight, we've got to do something.

The loud and sudden sound of a chainsaw starting up comes from the roof.

MAXINE: *(yelling over the noise)* Who's on the roof with a chainsaw?

After a while of loud sawing, we hear the sound of the 1,400 pound cow crashing through the kitchen ceiling. We do not see the cow falling. It happens behind the hanging sheet. The chainsaw can still be heard.

DUANE: Jesus Christ!

MAXINE tries to hold onto a chair. The chair falls taking MAXINE with it. She lands on her rear, legs up in the air.

DUANE: You alright?

DUANE goes to MAXINE who is still on the floor.

DUANE: Are you hurt?

MAXINE is in shock.

DUANE: Talk to me, Max.

MAXINE: My, my hip...

DUANE: It hurts?

MAXINE: Yeah.

DUANE: Can you move?

MAXINE: Yes. I think so.

MAXINE gets up and dusts herself off, rubs her butt where she fell.

MAXINE: Are you OK?

DUANE: Yeah.

DUANE pulls aside the curtain to see inside the kitchen. The audience doesn't see the cow.

DUANE: What the hell.

MAXINE: *(looking in the kitchen)* God almighty.

BILLIE runs in followed by PRU. The chainsaw has stopped.

BILLIE: Everybody OK?

MAXINE: We're alright.

BILLIE goes to look in the kitchen. The others follow. All staring at the sight from the doorway.

MAXINE: Look at that.

BILLIE: She missed the stove.

MAXINE: A small blessing.

PRU: What a wreck.

DUANE: It's the Carson's cow alright.

BILLIE gets her phone and shoots photos of the scene.

MAXINE: *(to BILLIE)* Billie, stop, it's a bloody mess.

DUANE: No, it's a good idea. The insurance company will want photos.

BILLIE: You can see the reflection of the sky in her open eyes.

DUANE: Do you smell something?

MAXINE: She landed on a giant jar of pickles.

DUANE: Never a dill moment.

MAXINE looks at DUANE, trying not to smile.

BILLIE: Her eyes are beautiful.

MAXINE: *(to Billie)* Careful. Don't slip on the juice.

DUANE: We don't need a crane now, just a butcher.

BILLIE: *(looking up)* Dad?

JEREMIAH leans over and pokes his head through the hole in the ceiling. We see his face upside down.

PRU: Jeremiah!

MAXINE: What the heck are you doing up there?

JEREMIAH: *(drunk)* I told you I'd take care of it. I'd take care of the cow. I'm taking care—

MAXINE: —Come down from there. Put the chainsaw down.

JEREMIAH: *(swaying with the chainsaw in his hands)* What did you say? You're very far away.

JEREMIAH bends down, closer to the hole in the roof.

PRU: *(to JEREMIAH)* Don't move! Stay right where you are.

DUANE: He's drunk.

PRU: Help him, for god's sake!

MAXINE: *(to DUANE)* Get him down, Duane, please. He must have used the ladder. Damn fool.

JEREMIAH and DUANE enter the diner.

MAXINE: Are you drunk, Jeremiah?

BILLIE starts filming the scene.

JEREMIAH: Maybe. I thought if I could push her, get her to gently roll off the roof then we wouldn't need a crane. Then I thought, no, what I need is—

BILLIE: —a chainsaw?

JEREMIAH: Yeah! I can do almost anything with a chainsaw. See!

PRU: Duane, grab that chainsaw, please!

DUANE grabs the chainsaw.

MAXINE: You could have gotten hurt.

JEREMIAH: The cow had to go. For the party. For the diner. For you, Max. *(to PRU)* Why are you crying?

DUANE: She's happy to see you.

JEREMIAH: *(to MAXINE)* I love this place. *(to the others)* Why is she crying?

BILLIE: We thought you were dead.

MAXINE: Billie!

BILLIE: What?

JEREMIAH: *(to PRU)* Don't leave me.

PRU: I am not going to leave you.

JEREMIAH: You're going down the Mississippi in a boat, that's what you said.

PRU: I never wanted to go down the Mississippi. I just wanted to do something to make you happy.

JEREMIAH: I'm happy here.

JEREMIAH sits himself down on the floor of the diner.

JEREMIAH: Here.

BILLIE: On the floor?

PRU: *(pulling JEREMIAH up)* Come on, honey, get up.

JEREMIAH: No, heeeerrreee.

JEREMIAH spins around, pointing his finger at the diner as he twirls and stumbles.

BILLIE: Hold on there, cowboy.

BILLIE helps PRU steady JEREMIAH.

DUANE starts making some coffee.

JEREMIAH: *(to PRU)* You were cleaning off that table there. You had on cut-offs and a Red Hot Chili Peppers t-shirt.

PRU: What?

JEREMIAH: You looked so hot.

PRU: Take my hand.

JEREMIAH: The music was loud. Lots of folks. Your Dad gave me $20 to bring the beer in from his, uh, ...truck. My first job.

BILLIE: This is where you guys met?

JEREMIAH: *(unsteady on his feet)* You smiled. Fireworks!

PRU: The Fourth of July party.

JEREMIAH: Boom!

BILLIE: *(under her breath)* Somebody is wasted.

BILLIE laughs.

PRU: *(smiles)* Boom!

BILLIE: *(to PRU)* How old were you?

PRU: Sixteen.

JEREMIAH: *(trying to hug PRU)* Sweet sixteen! And so beautiful. She wanted to be a dancer. A beautiful dancer. So graceful.

BILLIE: Really?

JEREMIAH tries again to twirl but almost falls.

PRU: Why don't you sit down right here? I'll get you some coffee.

You can hear the sound of cars approaching. BILLIE looks out the window. DUANE hands some coffee to PRU to give to JEREMIAH.

BILLIE: We might have some company.

MAXINE: What do you mean?

BILLIE: I see some cars coming.

MAXINE: They're probably lost.

PRU: *(rushing to the window)* They're parking.

MAXINE: Put the 'Closed' sign up. We can't serve anyone today.

DUANE: Isn't that the Lang family? And the Andersons?

MAXINE: What?

DUANE: They must have driven up all the way from Florida. I'll be damned.

PRU: Oh my God, I didn't send out the email.

MAXINE: You didn't cancel the party?

PRU: I had a lot on my mind.

MAXINE: Billie, get everything outside.

JEREMIAH: Party!

MAXINE: *(to BILLIE)* Don't forget the decorations.

BILLIE: Yes, m'am.

MAXINE: *(to DUANE)* Keep the coffee flowing over there *(pointing to JEREMIAH).* And close the curtain to the kitchen.

DUANE pulls the curtain closed and goes outside.

PRU: *(looking out the window)* There's Father Bob with his widow brigade. I don't know who some of those people are. Wow.

MAXINE: And I didn't think that anyone would come.

PRU: *(softly to herself)* I didn't either.

MAXINE: *(to PRU)* What?

PRU: *(still at the window)* No, it's amazing.

DUANE: You should go outside. There's quite a crowd forming.

MAXINE: Help me grab everything edible in the kitchen?

DUANE: *(picking up the chainsaw)* Everything?

MAXINE: Put that thing down.

DUANE grabs some food and goes outside.

MAXINE: *(to BILLIE)* Hon, bring that table and some chairs outside.

BILLIE and MAXINE take a table and some chairs outside. PRU sits down next to JEREMIAH.

PRU: You had me scared.

PRU holding JEREMIAH's hands.

PRU: I thought I'd lost you.

JEREMIAH: *(sobering up)* I'm sorry.

PRU fights back some tears.

JEREMIAH: Last night your Mom asked me a really good question.

PRU: You were with my Mom last night?

JEREMIAH: Before I fell asleep in the truck. I helped her close up the diner.

PRU: Funny that she didn't tell me that.

JEREMIAH: She asked me if I like farming.

PRU: What did you say?

JEREMIAH: I said it doesn't matter. But, Pru, it does matter. Here it is. Here's the truth. I don't like farming. You have every reason to be mad but I've got to be honest with you and myself. And I know I'm disappointing you. Your husband is a failure. I understand you wanting to leave me.

PRU: You idiot.

JEREMIAH: I know. I am a total idiot.

PRU: Listen to me. You're not a failure. And you are certainly not disappointing me. You're being truthful with yourself. Finally.

JEREMIAH: Yeah.

PRU: Yeah.

(BEAT)

PRU: So now what? Sell the farm?

JEREMIAH: That's a start.

PRU: Cruise down the Mississippi?

JEREMIAH: Before we do that, I have another idea.

PRU: What?

JEREMIAH: Why don't we buy the diner?

PRU: I can't cook, remember?

JEREMIAH: But I can.

PRU: What will I do?

JEREMIAH: Anything you want. Billie is going to college. Your Mom can retire.

PRU: Imagine.

JEREMIAH: You could help me fix up the diner. You've got great taste. Or maybe you go back to school?

PRU: And learn how to make coconut cakes.

JEREMIAH: That would free up space in the freezer.

PRU: *(Looking out the window.)* Shut up! *(Pause)* Maybe I could revitalize Dad's vegetable garden. Plant some fruit, some herbs. We could become the first farm to table road diner.

JEREMIAH: Farm to table? Isn't everything here farm to table?

JEREMIAH stands behind PRU at the window and hugs her. She turns to him.

PRU: You're smiling.

SCENE 9

Later that night. MAXINE and BILLIE are sitting at the counter in the diner. MAXINE opens two cans of soda.

BILLIE: It was pretty awesome.

MAXINE: Yes, it was.

BILLIE: You're a rock star, Gram.

MAXINE: Hush.

BILLIE: No, really. All those folks coming here because of you.

MAXINE: It's not me. It's the place.

BILLIE: Oh, don't be all humble now.

MAXINE takes a sip and sits quietly.

BILLIE: Gram, I'm going to California.

MAXINE: You're going to the fancy art college?

BILLIE: Yep.

MAXINE: And what about your, uh, situation?

BILLIE: I made a decision. A hard one. There's a clinic in California. I'm going to make an appointment.

MAXINE: Does that mean what I think it means?

BILLIE: Probably—maybe. I'm sorry, Gram—

MAXINE: No, it's your decision. I have to respect that.

MAXINE puts her hand over BILLIE's hand and nods her head.

MAXINE: Your folks are going to miss you. I'm going to miss you.

BILLIE: You guys are going to be crazy busy fixing up this joint. Mom told me about your plans.

MAXINE: I'll be supervising from that hammock outside, with a lemonade in one hand—

BILLIE: And a whip in the other?

MAXINE: Sounds about right.

DUANE enters the diner, carrying some chairs.

DUANE: That's all of the chairs. I'll get the tables tomorrow.

MAXINE: Thank you.

DUANE: What a shindig!

BILLIE: Wasn't it? Gram's a rock star.

MAXINE: Enough already. Guess who's going to California?

DUANE: Who?

MAXINE: Our Billie. She got accepted to a fancy art college in Los Angeles.

DUANE: That's amazing, kiddo! Congratulations!

BILLIE: Thank you!

DUANE: Los Angeles? That's right on the Pacific Ocean, right?

BILLIE: Yep.

DUANE: You want a ride?

MAXINE AND BILLIE: What?

BILLIE: You want to drive me to Los Angeles?

DUANE: Yeah. I want to see the Pacific Ocean.

MAXINE: You're really serious?

DUANE: I'm serious. No joke.

BILLIE: That would be awesome!

DUANE: Excellent.

BILLIE: A road trip!

MAXINE: So how long will it take you to get to Los Angeles?

BILLIE: According to Google Maps, it is approximately 1,552 miles.

MAXINE: And that's how many days?

DUANE: A couple, give or take a few.

MAXINE: Is there room for another passenger?

DUANE: What? Do you want to come? Really?

BILLIE: You'd leave the diner?

MAXINE: Not much for me to do here while they renovate.

DUANE: Tomorrow, I'll buy us a map.

BILLIE: The map's right here, old man. *(Showing DUANE her phone with Google Maps.)*

DUANE: No way, I'm old-school.

BILLIE: Maybe on the trip Duane will sing your birthday song for us?

MAXINE: What birthday song?

BILLIE: The one he wrote for you, or should I say Grandpa wrote for you?

MAXINE: Oh, my Lord, did you tell her that story?

BILLIE: Yes, he did. Great story.

MAXINE: It is.

BILLIE: Come on, sing the song.

DUANE: Speaking of great stories, there's this moth who goes to see a podiatrist—

BILLIE: —Oh my God!

DUANE: And he tells the doctor, you can't believe what's been happening. First off, my wife left me. We have been together twenty-two years and she up and leaves. Leaves me for the guy who sells jam—

BILLIE: —Wasn't it honey?

DUANE: Right! She leaves me for this guy who sells honey in the local farmers' market. She tells her friends terrible things about me. And my kids, well, what spiteful little brats. All they want from me is money. They never come to visit. I sit in my little apartment all alone, just watching stupid tv shows. My life has become so empty and meaningless. And the doctor says, 'I am so sorry for all the hard things you must be going through.' You don't know the half of it, doc, the moth says.

Then they found some creepy mold in my apartment. The doctor interrupted him again. 'I understand but I must ask, why did you come to see me? I am a podiatrist. I treat people's feet.' And the moth looks up at him, confused by the stupidity of the question, and says, I came to you, doc, because your light was on.

END

ALSO AVAILABLE FROM SALAMANDER STREET

All Salamander Street plays can be bought in bulk at a discount for performance or study. Contact info@salamanderstreet.com to enquire about performance licenses.

THE GLASGOW POISONER
by Tom Cooper & Jen McGregor
ISBN: 9781068233456

A gripping new true crime musical inspired by the sensational 19th-century murder trial of Madeleine Smith, blending historical scandal, courtroom drama and darkly comic musical theatre.

PLACEHOLDER by Catherine Bisset
ISBN: 9781068696282

A parallel text version of Catherine Bisset's dramatic solo play set in 1790 Saint-Domingue – the daughter of an enslaved woman reflects on her life as an opera singer and the importance of resistance.

EAT THE RICH (BUT MAYBE NOT ME MATES X)
by Jade Franks
ISBN: 9781068233449

A sharp, funny look at class, identity and friendship. Jade Franks's award-winning solo show asks "What happens when a Liverpool girl crashes the Cambridge bubble?" Called the 'new Fleabag' by The Times.

GROUP PORTRAIT IN A SUMMER LANDSCAPE
by Peter Arnott
ISBN: 9781914228933

An intense and riveting play set in a Perthshire country house during the Scottish Independence referendum of 2014. A retired academic and political heavyweight invites family and former students together for a dramatic reckoning.

Salamander Street